DISCOVERING ANCIENT MESOAMERICAN CIVILIZATIONS

DISCOVERING ANCIENT MESOAMERICAN CIVILIZATIONS

ANN BYERS

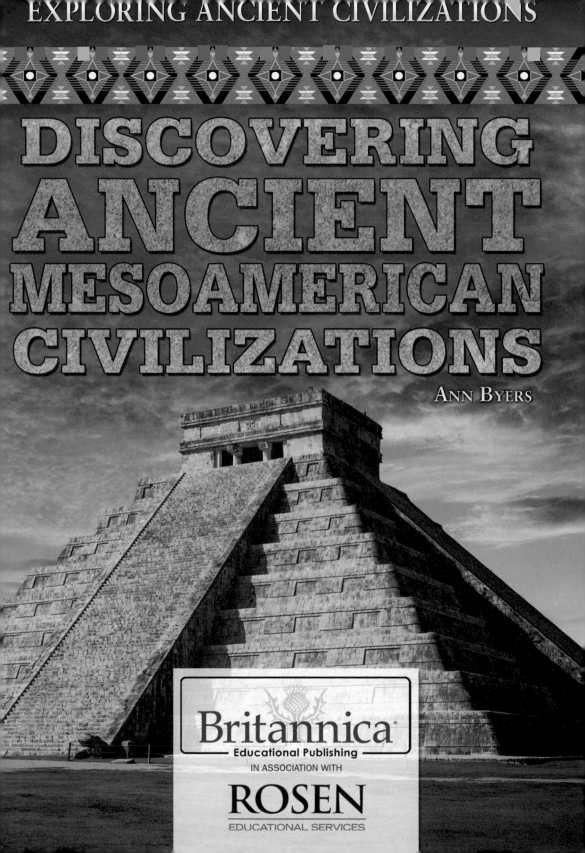

Britannica®
Educational Publishing

IN ASSOCIATION WITH

ROSEN
EDUCATIONAL SERVICES

Published in 2015 by Britannica Educational Publishing (a trademark of Encyclopædia Britannica, Inc.) in association with The Rosen Publishing Group, Inc.
29 East 21st Street, New York, NY 10010

Distributed exclusively by Rosen Publishing.
To see additional Britannica Educational Publishing titles, go to http://wwww.rosenpublishing.com.

First Edition

Britannica Educational Publishing
J. E. Luebering: Director, Core Reference Group
Anthony L. Green: Editor, Compton's by Britannica

Rosen Publishing
Kathy Campbell: Editor
Nelson Sá: Art Director
Brian Garvey: Designer
Cindy Reiman: Photography Manager

Library of Congress Cataloging-in-Publication Data

Byers, Ann, author.
Discovering ancient Mesoamerican civilizations/Ann Byers.—First edition.
       pages cm.— (Exploring ancient civilizations)
Includes bibliographical references and index.
ISBN 978-1-62275-841-8 (library bound)—ISBN 978-1-62275-842-5 (pbk.)—
ISBN 978-1-62275-843-2 (6-pack)
1. Indians of Mexico—Juvenile literature. 2. Indians of Central America—Juvenile literature. I. Title. II. Series: Exploring ancient civilizations.
F1219.B985 2015
930—dc23

                                                                                2014025498

Manufactured in the United States of America

Photo credits: Cover, pp. 1, 3 Jose Ignacio Soto/Shutterstock.com; pp. 7, 14 Encyclopædia Britannica, Inc.; pp. 9, 17, 23, 27 De Agostini/Getty Images; p. 10 © Danita Delimont/Alamy; p. 12 Jacobo Zanella/ Moment Open/Getty Images; p. 13 DEA/C. Sappa/De Agostini/Getty Images; p. 18 DEA/G. Dagli Orti/ De Agostini/Getty Images; p. 19 Danita Delimont/Gallo Images/Getty Images; p. 21 Private Collection/ Bridgeman Images; p. 25 Dorling Kindersley/Getty Images; p. 28 Richard Maschmeyer/Robert Harding World Imagery/Getty Images; p. 30 The Bridgeman Art Library/Getty Images; pp. 31, 37 Werner Forman/ Universal Images Group/Getty Images; p. 32 BornaMir/iStock/Thinkstock; p. 33 Library of Congress, Washington, D.C. (neg. no. LC-USZC4-73); p. 36 Maxime Vige/E+/Getty Images; p. 39 George Holton/ Photo Researchers; p. 41 Michael & Jennifer Lewis/National Geographic Image Collection/Getty Images; p. 42 Independent Picture Service/Universal Images Group/Getty; cover and interior graphics to mua to/Shutterstock.com (patterned banners and borders), HorenkO/Shutterstock.com and Freckles/ Shutterstock.com (background textures).

CONTENTS

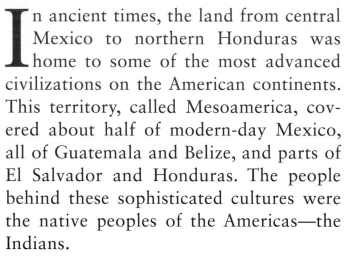

INTRODUCTION

In ancient times, the land from central Mexico to northern Honduras was home to some of the most advanced civilizations on the American continents. This territory, called Mesoamerica, covered about half of modern-day Mexico, all of Guatemala and Belize, and parts of El Salvador and Honduras. The people behind these sophisticated cultures were the native peoples of the Americas—the Indians.

Much like in ancient Egypt, Mesopotamia, and China, the Indians of Mesoamerica advanced from primitive ways to complex societies. Beginning with almost nothing, they eventually established elaborate cities, built massive monuments, and created beautiful works of art. They learned how to grow food in tropical rain forests and on mountain slopes. They developed customs and laws and made amazing discoveries in astronomy and math.

What were these ancient people like? What did they believe? How did they

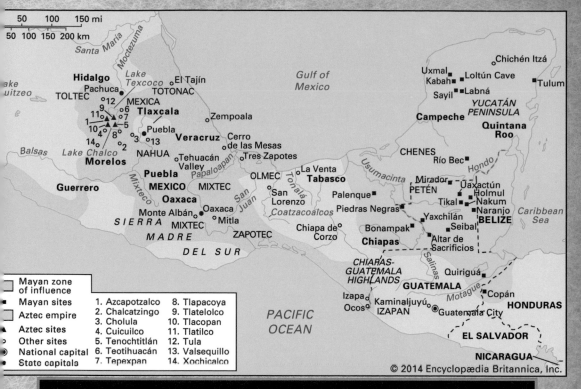

| 50 | 100 | 150 mi |
| 50 | 100 | 150 | 200 km |

Santa María
Moctezuma
Hidalgo
ake uitzeo
Lake Texcoco
El Tajín
Pachuca
TOTONAC
TOLTEC
MEXICA
12
Tlaxcala
9
6
7
Zempoala
11
10
5
Puebla
14
4
8
3
13
Veracruz
Cerro de las Mesas
2
NAHUA
Tehuacán
Tres Zapotes
Morelos
Valley
Papaloapan
La Venta
Balsas
Lake Chalco
Puebla
OLMEC
Tabasco
Guerrero
MEXICO
MIXTEC
San Juan
San Lorenzo
Palenque
Oaxaca
Tonalá
Coatzacoalcos
Piedras Negras
Monte Albán
Oaxaca
Mitla
SIERRA
MIXTEC
ZAPOTEC
Chiapa de Corzo
Bonampak
MADRE
Chiapas
Altar de Sacrificios
DEL SUR
CHIAPAS-GUATEMALA HIGHLANDS
Mixteco

Gulf of Mexico

Uxmal
Chichén Itzá
Kabah
Loltún Cave
Sayil
Labná
Tulum
Campeche
YUCATÁN PENINSULA
Quintana Roo
CHENES
Río Bec
Hondo
Usumacinta
Mirador
Uaxactún
PETÉN
Holmul
Tikal
Nakum
Yaxchilán
Naranjo
Seibal
BELIZE
Caribbean Sea
Quiriguá
GUATEMALA
Motagua
Copán
Izapa
Kaminaljuyú
HONDURAS
Ocos
IZAPAN
Guatemala City
EL SALVADOR
NICARAGUA
Salinas

PACIFIC OCEAN

	Mayan zone of influence		
	Mayan sites	1. Azcapotzalco	8. Tlapacoya
	Aztec empire	2. Chalcatzingo	9. Tlatelolco
	Aztec sites	3. Cholula	10. Tlacopan
	Other sites	4. Cuicuilco	11. Tlatilco
	National capital	5. Tenochtitlán	12. Tula
	State capitals	6. Teotihuacán	13. Valsequillo
		7. Tepexpan	14. Xochicalco

© 2014 Encyclopædia Britannica, Inc.

This map shows the locations of ancient and modern cities in Mesoamerica. In addition to the Aztec and the Maya, the Olmec, Zapotec, Toltec, and other peoples developed civilizations in this area in ancient times.

live? Fortunately, they left records. The records are the items they made: their buildings, their artwork, and their picture writing. From these, archaeologists have pieced together a picture of fascinating people who began to civilize the continent more than 3,000 years ago.

7

CHAPTER ONE

THE STORY OF MESOAMERICA

T he first people to come to Mesoamerica were hunter-gatherers. Hunter-gatherers live in small, family-based groups called bands, which move from place to place looking for food. They kill wild animals and collect the fruit of edible plants. When they exhaust the supply in one location, they move to another. They continue this nomadic way of life until they figure out how to grow food. Once they learn to farm, life changes dramatically. They no longer have to move; they settle, forming small villages.

Because they spend less time getting food, they can pursue other activities. They find ways to use the resources in their environment to make their lives easier and more enjoyable. Over time they develop a division of labor; some people concentrate on farming and others make pots, baskets, jewelry, and other items. When people cooperate on projects, they develop rules for working together. The villages eventually grow into cities, the rules into laws, and the division of labor into social classes. These developments are some of the characteristics of a civilization.

The rise from farming to civilization can take thousands of years. In Mesoamerica, Indians began to experiment with raising plants as early as 8000 BCE. By 5000 BCE they had begun using corn as a food. Squash, beans,

Mesoamerican farmers dug holes and planted single seeds of corn, beans, and squash together in each hole. The corn provided stalks for the bean plants to climb, and the corn and beans shaded the squash, which grew close to the ground.

and chili peppers were other early crops. By 1500 BCE some Mesoamerican farmers were producing enough food that the people were ready to live a fully settled life.

The Mother Culture: The Olmec

The first great civilization in Mesoamerica was that of the Olmec. These people settled along the hot, humid coast of the Gulf of Mexico in what are today the Mexican states of Veracruz and Tabasco. By about 1200 BCE their simple farming villages had evolved into a civilization.

The Olmec built large towns where they came together to trade and hold religious ceremonies. The most important were San Lorenzo, La Venta, and Tres Zapotes. San Lorenzo, the oldest site, is famous for its extraordinary stone monuments. La Venta is marked by great

The Olmec settlement of La Venta, on the Gulf coast of Mexico, was originally built on an island in the Tonalá River. Today it is part of a large swamp. A 100-foot- (30-meter-) high clay mound, shaped like a fluted cone, towers over the site. Some archaeologists believe that it represents a volcano.

mounds, a narrow plaza, and several other ceremonial enclosures. Between about 800 and 400 BCE it was the most important settlement in Mesoamerica.

Olmec culture faded by about 400 BCE. Its influence, however, spread north to central Mexico and south to Central America.

Classic Civilizations

As the Olmec declined, other civilizations rose. Several reached their peak during what is called the Classic era of ancient Mesoamerican civilization. This period lasted from about 100 to 900 CE.

The Zapotec made their home in the mountains of southern Mexico. In about 500 BCE they established a political and cultural center at Monte Albán, near the present-day city of Oaxaca. The ancient city had pyramids, temples, elaborate tombs, underground passageways, and a ball court. Monte Albán reached its height between 300 and 900 CE. After that, Zapotec influence declined as the Mixtec civilization ascended.

As Monte Albán flourished in Oaxaca, Teotihuacán emerged in central Mexico.

The photograph shows a view of Teotihuacán from the top of the Pyramid of the Sun, the third-largest pyramid in the world.

Located near present-day Mexico City, it was the greatest city in the Americas before the arrival of Europeans. At its height in about 500 CE, it may have housed more than 150,000 people. At the time it was one of the largest cities in the world. Teotihuacán contained great plazas, temples, palaces of nobles and priests, and some 2,000 single-story apartment compounds. Its culture spread throughout much of Mesoamerica. Around 750 CE the main part of the city burned, possibly in a rebellion or a civil war.

Although parts of the city were occupied after that event, much of it fell into ruin.

While these cultures rose and fell in the highlands, the Maya established a great civilization in the lowlands of what are now southern Mexico, Guatemala, Belize, and Honduras. By about 250 CE the villages of the Maya had developed into cities containing temples, pyramids, palaces, ball courts, and plazas. At its height, Mayan civilization consisted of more than 40 cities, each with a population between 5,000 and 50,000.

Among the main cities were Tikal, Copán, Bonampak, Palenque, and Río Bec. The peak Mayan population may have reached 2 million people.

The great Mayan cities of the lowlands declined after 900 CE. No one knows why, though warfare and the exhaustion of farmland may have

This tower in Chichén Itzá, rising high above the trees, was a Mayan observatory. Archaeologists named it El Caracol—"the snail"—because of its spiral stairway.

DIVINE DIRECTION

According to Aztec legend, the god Huitzilopochtli led the Aztec to a sacred place where they could settle. He told them to look for an eagle sitting on a cactus eating a snake. After much wandering, the people saw this sign on an island in Lake Texcoco. There they built their capital, Tenochtitlán. The emblem on Mexico's flag and official seal—featuring an eagle, a cactus, and a snake—depicts the myth of the city's founding.

The Mexican flag shows the scene that the founders of Tenochtitlán supposedly saw—an eagle with a snake in its beak standing on a cactus growing on an island.

played a role. After 900, Mayan cities such as Chichén Itzá, Uxmal, and Mayapán continued to flourish on the Yucatán Peninsula for hundreds more years.

Postclassic Civilizations

The final period of ancient Mesoamerican history is called the Postclassic ("post-"

means "after"). It lasted from about 900 to 1519, when the Spanish conqueror Hernán Cortés arrived.

From about 900 to the mid-1100s the Toltec people had the most powerful and culturally advanced civilization in central Mexico. Toltec culture centered on their capital, Tula, which was not far from modern-day Mexico City. Tula probably had a population in the tens of thousands. The heart of the city consisted of a large plaza bordered on one side by a temple pyramid, which was probably dedicated to the god Quetzalcóatl, the Feathered Serpent.

The Toltec controlled central Mexico until the Aztec invaded from the north, destroying Tula around 1150. In the 1400s and early 1500s the Aztec built an empire that dominated the region until the Spanish arrived. At its height, the Aztec Empire had a population of five to six million people. The capital of the empire was Tenochtitlán, on the site of Mexico City. In 1521 Cortés and his army destroyed the city and conquered the Aztec, ending the last of the ancient civilizations.

CHAPTER TWO
LIFE IN MESOAMERICA

The ancient civilizations of Mesoamerica spanned 2,700 years and thrived in a great variety of landscapes and environments. Yet they had much in common, in part because of their common Olmec heritage. There were similarities in their economies, their social organization, and their customs.

Agriculture

Agriculture was the base of Mesoamerican civilizations. The Indians planted a great many crops, of which corn (maize), beans, and squash were the most important. Others included chili peppers, tomatoes, sweet potatoes, manioc, cotton, cacao, pineapples, papayas, peanuts, and avocados. The types of crops grown in a particular area depended mostly on the environment. The environment, in turn, depended on the area's geography—whether it was in the highlands or the lowlands. Because many crops could be raised only in certain places, trade between regions became common.

The most productive fields were in the highlands, where farmers used a variety of special techniques. In places with sloping land, farmers created terraces to control erosion. The terraces were level plots built into the sides of hills or mountains in a stepped pattern. They were made of either earth and maguey (a hard fiber taken from the agave plant) or stone. In some places people built irrigation canals to carry water to their fields.

Besides corn, beans, and squash, Mesoamerican farmers planted chili peppers, tomatoes, cacao, peanuts, and avocados, among other edible plants. These drawings from a 16th-century Spanish manuscript depict Aztec farmers harvesting crops.

Mesoamericans made *chinampas* by driving poles into the lake bed, weaving rafts of branches and reeds, and filling them with mud and vegetation. They traveled between the artificial islands by boat.

A unique feature of Mesoamerican highland agriculture was the use of *chinampas*. These artificial islands were built up above the surface of a shallow lake using mud and plants from the lake floor. After settling, the *chinampa* was a rich planting bed. Tenochtitlán, the Aztec capital, depended on *chinampas* for much of its food.

In the lowlands, Mesoamericans typically practiced slash-and-burn farming. Toward the end of the dry season, they selected a patch of forest for planting. Next, they removed a band of bark from the trunks of larger trees (the "slash"), which caused the tree to die and shed its leaves. Then they burned and cleared away the undergrowth and smaller trees. The new field was ready to be planted in time for the first rains. After a few years of planting, the fertility of the

NEW WORLD WORDS

When the Spaniards came to America, they discovered many new things. One of the surprises was chocolate. They adopted the Aztec words for chocolate and cocoa. They also adopted Aztec words for other foods native to Mesoamerica: tomato, avocado, and jicama. Other words that people think of as Spanish also came from Aztec: tamale, guacamole, and chili. In addition to terms for foods, the Aztec gave English speakers the words "mesquite," "shack," "ocelot," and "coyote."

This ceramic figure depicts a woman holding a goblet of chocolate. Mesoamericans believed chocolate was a gift from the Feathered Serpent.

soil declined, weeds increased, and the field was abandoned to the forest.

Later, the Maya and other lowland peoples developed raised-field agriculture. They dug canals through the swamps, piling up the dirt to create dry plots for planting. These fields were similar to the *chinampas* of the highlands. The canals were used for irrigation. Farmers also constructed terraces in some lowland regions.

Diet

The diet was similar throughout Mesoamerica. The Indians boiled dried corn to soften the hull and then ground it into cornmeal. They used dough made of cornmeal and water to make thin, flat bread called tortillas. The tortillas were eaten with sauces prepared from chili peppers and tomatoes, along with boiled beans. They also mixed ground corn with water to make a drink called posol. At higher altitudes they made pulque, an alcoholic drink, from the fermented sap of the maguey plant.

Luxury foods included cocoa drinks, meats, and fish. Meat came from deer or from small game such as rabbits and raccoons. The Mesoamericans also kept dogs and turkeys for food. These were the only two animals that the Indians raised.

Society

The civilizations of Meso-america were the first in the Americas to be divided into social classes. A person's position in the class system was based on wealth and status. Throughout Mesoamerica, the rulers and the nobles were believed to have been created separately from commoners. They formed the upper class, or the elite. This class included the priests, who were powerful authority figures.

Social classes emerged early in Meso-america. The first Olmec settlements were agricul-tural villages with a simple social order. Because all the people were farmers, they

EXTRACTING PULQUE.

A 19th-century engraving shows a man extracting sap from a maguey plant to make the drink called pulque.

COUNTERFEIT BEANS

The Aztec market at Tlatelolco, sister city of Tenochtitlán, was huge. On major market days, as many as 60,000 people bought and sold goods there. The medium of exchange for small items was the cocoa bean. A tomato sold for one bean, an avocado for three. You could buy a rabbit with 30 beans and a turkey hen with 100. Some people tried to cheat. Some opened the cocoa bean shells and replaced the beans with mud; others made counterfeit beans out of wax or dough.

were not ranked in social classes. But within a few hundred years the Olmec began to build large pyramids and carve huge stone sculptures. These changes show that different social classes had developed. Only powerful leaders could have commanded craftsmen and laborers to create such monumental works. In addition, the sculptures are thought to depict chiefs or rulers.

The social system grew more complex in later civilizations. The Maya had a highly organized society in which the work of peasant farmers freed the nobility and the priests from daily drudgery in the fields. The elite used the extra time to build the cities, pyramids, and temples and to pursue intellectual studies. The social structure of the Maya was reflected in their cities. The ruins of Tikal, the mightiest Maya center of all, include about 3,000 structures. They range from tiny mounds on which common people built their simple pole-and-thatch dwellings up to gigantic temple pyramids and palaces for the upper class.

Aztec society was also based on a complex hierarchy. At the top was the ruling class, similar to that of the Maya. At the bottom were the serfs and slaves. Serfs worked on private and state-owned rural estates; slaves were used mostly for human sacrifice. A man could move up in class through promotions, usually as a reward for courage in war. Women were similarly rewarded for

These 16th-century drawings by a Spanish monk show Aztec artisans processing feathers for headdresses, shields, and other items. Feather workers were not allowed to wear their creations; they were for nobles and rulers only.

braving the dangers of childbirth. Certain occupations—such as merchants, gold-smiths, and feather workers—were given more prestige than others.

The Ball Game

The sport known simply as the ball game was played by Indians throughout Mesoamerica. It originated among the Olmec or possibly even earlier. Then it spread to other cultures, among them the Zapotec, the Maya (who called it *pok-ta-pok*), the Toltec, and the Aztec. Some of the best-preserved ball courts of Mesoamerica can be seen at the Zapotec site of Monte Albán and the Mayan cities of Chichén Itzá and Copán.

The game took place on an I-shaped court with high walls on the long sides. Players, wearing heavy padding, used elbows, knees, and hips to knock a solid rubber ball into the opponent's end of the court. In later years—after about 900 CE—the object was to hit the ball through one of two stone rings attached to the wall, one on each side of the court.

The game had religious significance. Various myths mention it, sometimes as a contest between day and night gods. The court represented the heavens. The ball represented the Sun (or Moon or stars), and the rings represented the sunrise and sunset or the equinoxes. The game was extremely violent and often caused serious injury and, occasionally, death. In addition, the captain of the losing team, and sometimes the entire team, may have been sacrificed to the gods.

Balls for this ritual ball game were made of rubber, a substance unknown in Europe until the discovery of the Americas. Variations of the game are still played in parts of Mexico.

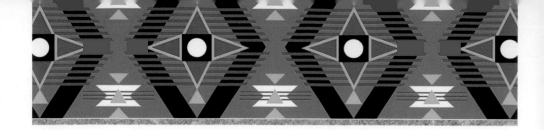

CHAPTER THREE

MESOAMERICAN RELIGION

The early Mesoamericans tried to understand how their world "worked." What made the Sun come up each day? Where did wind come from? How did water fall from the sky? They decided that unseen forces, or gods, controlled everything. They developed a worldview—a particular way of looking at the world.

Worldview

To early Mesoamericans, the world had three layers: the earth, thirteen heavens, and nine underworlds. Each of the heavens and the underworlds had a ruling god. The heavens and the underworlds were not like the Christian ideas of heaven and hell. They were not places of good and evil, but of light and dark. The afterlife had nothing to do with how people lived on earth. After death, most people traveled through the nine underworlds. Only a few groups of people went to the heavens, including warriors who died in battle and women who died in childbirth.

Many Mesoamerican peoples believed that several worlds had been created and destroyed before the present universe had come into being. The Aztec, for example, believed the gods had created five worlds, called suns.

This Aztec depiction of the world shows Xiuhtecuhtli, the god of fire, at the center. He is facing north with south behind him, east above, and west at his feet.

The first four suns had been destroyed by catastrophes created by the gods. The present world was the fifth sun, and the Aztec thought of themselves as "the People of the Sun." Their divine duty was to nourish the Sun so it would not disappear from the heavens. Thus the welfare and the very survival of the universe depended upon offerings of blood and hearts to the Sun.

A GOD RETURNS

This stone carving on the Temple of Quetzalcóatl in Teotihuacán is one of many throughout Mesoamerica that depict the head of the Feathered Serpent.

In one Aztec story, the great god Quetzalcóatl appears in human form as a light-skinned, bearded man. He is tricked by another god and leaves the city of Tula (or Tollan) on a raft made out of snakes. He vows to return at a certain time. That time translated to the year 1519 on the European calendar. When the Spanish soldier Hernán Cortés arrived in Mexico in that year on a boat, the Aztec thought he was Quetzalcóatl returning to them. They welcomed the man who eventually destroyed their civilization.

Religious authority among the Mesoamericans was in the hands of the priests. Priests were usually astronomers. They charted the movements of the heavenly bodies and assigned days in the calendar to specific gods. The astronomer-priests told the people what the god of the day required.

Gods

Ancient Mesoamericans had many gods. Their religion emphasized the Sun, the Moon, and other heavenly bodies, and these were represented by gods. There were gods who created the universe and invented human culture. There were gods for basic activities such as war, hunting, and agriculture. There were also gods of craft groups, social classes, and political systems. Some gods were believed to control more than one realm. Huitzilopochtli, a main god of the Aztec, was god of both the Sun and war.

Certain gods were found throughout Mesoamerica. Every culture had a corn god, for example, because corn was one of the most important things in the lives of the ancient people. The Olmec corn god was pictured with corn growing from the top of his head. The rain god was also very important because rain was essential to agriculture. Among the Toltec, the Aztec, and the people of Teotihuacán, the rain god was called Tlaloc. The name of the Zapotec rain god was Cocijo, and the Mayan rain god was Chac. This

This ceramic incense burner depicts Chac, the Mayan rain god. He is sometimes pictured with a long nose and fangs. Here he holds a bowl of smoking incense.

god could bring gentle showers or storms and lightning. He could send rain or withhold it.

The Mesoamericans often depicted their gods with animal characteristics. The Aztec represented Huitzilopochtli as either a hummingbird or an eagle. The Olmec gods were a cross between jaguar and human infant, often crying or snarling with open mouth. This "were-jaguar" appears widely in Olmec art.

This jade figurine of a jaguar spirit has typical Olmec facial features: a flat nose, thick lips, a down-turned mouth, and narrow eyes.

The Feathered Serpent was worshipped throughout the area. He appears on an Olmec carving, and a temple in Teotihuacán was dedicated to him. In those cultures, he was a vegetation god. In later cultures, the Feathered Serpent became the god of the morning and evening star. His disappearance and reappearance in the sky represented death and rebirth. The Toltec and the Aztec called this god Quetzalcóatl; the Maya named him Kukulcán.

EQUINOX OF THE RATTLESNAKE

Twice every year the god Kukulcán appears to visit his temple in the ancient Mayan city of Chichén Itzá. It happens on the two equinoxes—the first day of spring and the first day of autumn. On those days the afternoon sun and shadows create seven triangles on the temple pyramid's main staircase. The shadows resemble a rattlesnake slithering down the stairs from the top to the giant serpent's head at the bottom. The "visit" lasts about 10 minutes.

White triangles of sunlight appear on the staircase of Kukulcán's temple and then disappear from top to bottom as shadows shift, giving the appearance of a snake's movement.

Temple Pyramids and Sacrifice

Ancient Mesoamericans worshipped their gods in temples built on the flat tops of pyramids. These pyramids consisted of a series of rectangular platforms stacked on top of each other, each level smaller than the one beneath it. They were often built over caves, which perhaps represented entrances to the underworlds. The pyramids were tombs of important people. The temple was a place for worshipping the deceased leader, the gods from which he claimed descent, or both. Religious ceremonies featured processions, dances, and theatrical performances.

Another way Mesoamericans honored their gods was through sacrifice. They made constant offerings to the gods, including crops,

This Aztec drawing shows a priest atop a temple cutting hearts from live victims and offering them to Huitzilopochtli, the Sun and war god.

flowers, animals, rubber, and jade. Because they believed the gods needed blood for nourishment and strength, they practiced a form of self-sacrifice called bloodletting. They pierced themselves through the ears, tongues, or other body parts to get blood to offer the gods.

This type of worship reached its peak in the practice of human sacrifice, particularly among the Maya and the Aztec. They started wars with other Indians to acquire prisoners for the necessary sacrifices. The Aztec also bought slaves in lowland markets to use as victims. At Chichén Itzá the Maya hurled victims into a sacred cenote, a deep natural well, so the god Chac would send rain.

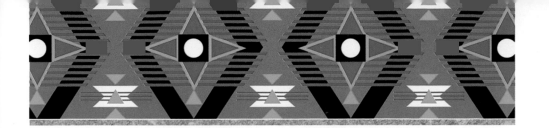

CHAPTER FOUR

ACHIEVEMENTS OF THE MESOAMERICANS

The civilizations of ancient Mesoamerica reached new heights in a number of areas. The pyramids, palaces, and other architectural wonders of their cities were among their greatest achievements. But they also made great strides in astronomy, calendar making, mathematics, writing, and the arts. Each of the Mesoamerican peoples developed their own strengths, typically building on the work of the cultures that came before. In the life of the mind, however, it was the achievements of the Maya that stood above all.

Astronomy and Mathematics

For the Mesoamericans, astronomy was closely tied to religion. Priests were the astronomers, and they watched the heavenly bodies because of their religious significance. The main purpose of their study was to learn what influence the heavens might have on human life.

The ruins of Palenque, a Mayan city in what is now the Mexican state of Chiapas, are covered with inscriptions that tell stories of people and events from the city's history.

The observations of the astronomer-priests were extraordinarily detailed and accurate. The Maya could trace the paths of the Moon and the planet Venus. They also correctly predicted solar eclipses.

Astronomical observations helped the Mesoamericans to create a complex and accurate calendar. It included a solar year of 365 days and a sacred year of 260 days. The same basic calendar was used throughout the region to schedule rituals and determine "good" and "bad" days for certain events. The calendar may have originated among the Olmec, but it was the Maya who perfected it.

In mathematics, the Mesoamericans developed two revolutionary concepts: place value and a way to represent zero. The Maya are usually credited with these achievements, but both appear in Olmec inscriptions centuries before the Maya.

Writing

The Mesoamericans invented their own forms of picture writing. The pictures were symbols that stood for words or sounds. The Indians used writing to record calendars, the names of rulers, and historical events.

The Olmec may have developed the first writing system in the Americas. In the late 20th century a stone slab engraved

This disc from the floor of a Mayan ball court at Chinkultic depicts a ball player. The symbols around the edges record the date the court was dedicated.

with pictures that appear to have been Olmec writing was discovered in the village of Cascajal, near the Olmec site of San Lorenzo. The Cascajal stone dates to about 900 BCE.

The Mayan writing system contained more than 800 symbols. When scholars first began studying Mayan writing, they thought that each symbol represented an entire word. Later they figured out that some symbols represented sounds. The symbols that stood for words were recognizable pictures of real things, such as animals, people, and objects of daily life.

Archaeologists have found Mesoamerican writing on buildings, stone slabs, sculpture, and pottery. After about 1000 CE the Maya and the Aztec made books. They wrote on long strips of deerskin, cotton cloth, or tree bark and folded the strips like an accordion. A great many of the ancient books were destroyed by the conquerors. The Spanish priests did not like the stories of the gods, and they ordered the books burned. Fortunately, a few survived to help archaeologists reconstruct what life must have been like in ancient Mesoamerica.

Arts

With agriculture providing a steady food supply, Mesoamerican civilizations were able to devote time to art. There was commonly a class of artisans who were responsible for both advanced stone architecture and for highly developed styles of sculpture, pottery, painting, metalwork, and other arts. Their art was often tied to their religion.

The Olmec introduced a style of art that influenced many later cultures. They may have been the greatest sculptors of ancient Mesoamerica. The artifacts they left range from huge stone sculptures to small jade carvings and pottery. Most striking are the "colossal heads," which are human portraits

COLOSSAL HEADS

The Olmec produced one form of art no other group copied: giant heads carved out of rock. Seventeen of these colossal heads have been found at four locations. The largest of them is more than 11 feet (3.4 meters) high. Each head was carved from a single piece of basalt. The Olmec had to bring the huge rocks from volcanic mountains more than 50 miles (80 kilometers) away. The heads have flat faces and helmet-like headgear. Each head is unique, probably made to look like a specific person. Archaeologists think the heads are portraits of Olmec rulers.

This 8-foot (2.4-meter) head found at La Venta, now Tabasco, was carved by Olmec craftsmen more than 2,500 years ago.

on a massive scale. These monuments are especially remarkable considering that the only carving methods available were pounding and pecking with stone tools.

In Teotihuacán, the walls of the palaces of noble families were magnificently painted with images of gods and myths. The people of Teotihuacán also produced distinctive pottery. Their most famous design is a cylinder-shaped vase with three legs and a cover. These vases were often painted with scenes like those on the walls of the buildings. There are also vessels shaped like flower vases and cream pitchers.

The Maya are also renowned for their art. They made pottery featuring designs of cranes, flying parrots, gods, and men. They also made beautiful murals, or wall paintings. In 1946 archaeologists were astounded by the colorful murals found in the Mayan city of Bonampak. The walls of one of its buildings are covered from floor to ceiling with colorful paintings of rituals, battles, and victory ceremonies.

The Toltec were known for their metalwork and sculpture. They made fine objects in gold, silver, and copper. Their sculptures included the Chac Mools—reclining male

Before the Temple of the Murals in Bonampak was discovered in 1946, historians thought the Maya were peaceful people. The paintings depict scenes of warfare and human sacrifice.

figures with a dish resting on the stomach. Thought to represent the rain god Chac, Chac Mools were probably used to hold the hearts of people sacrificed during religious ceremonies.

41

Conclusion

Chac Mools, such as the one pictured here in the Toltec city of Tula, originated among the Toltec and then spread to other Mesoamerican cultures.

The art, writing, and ruins left behind by the ancient Mesoamericans have told archaeologists much about the early civilizations of the New World. They have painted a picture of resourceful people who tamed their environments, built great cities, and accomplished scientific feats unknown in Europe at the time. Yet there is still more to be learned. The discovery of the Cascajal stone is one example of a recent finding that shows how our knowledge of the ancient Americas continues to unfold. Its ancient script has caused archaeologists to look anew at the Mesoamerican mother culture, the Olmec. To be sure, ongoing research will further illuminate the Olmec and the extraordinary civilizations that followed.

AFTERLIFE Existence after death.

ARCHAEOLOGIST A specialist in archaeology, the scientific study of bones, tools, and other objects left behind by ancient people.

ARTISAN A person who is skilled at making things by hand.

ASTRONOMY The scientific study of stars, planets, and other objects in outer space.

BASALT A dark gray to black rock formed by the cooling of a certain type of lava.

CANAL An artificial waterway used to carry water to farmland.

CENOTE A deep sinkhole in limestone that forms a natural well.

COLOSSAL Massive; of very great size.

COUNTERFEIT Not real; made in imitation of something else so as to deceive.

EQUINOX Either of the two times each year (about March 21 and September 23) when the Sun crosses the Equator and day and night are everywhere on Earth of approximately equal length.

EROSION The wearing away of land.

FERTILITY The ability to support the growth of many plants.

HIERARCHY A system in which people or things are placed in a series of levels with different importance or status.

INSCRIPTION Something that is written on or cut into a surface.

GLOSSARY

IRRIGATION The supply of water to farmland by artificial means.

MANIOC A tropical plant with a fleshy root that yields a nourishing starch. Also called cassava and yucca.

MEDIUM OF EXCHANGE Something commonly accepted in exchange for goods and services and recognized as representing a standard of value, such as money.

NOBLE A member of the nobility, which is the highest social class in some places.

NOMAD A person who moves from place to place instead of living in a fixed home.

PRESTIGE Respect and admiration.

RITUAL A ceremony or series of actions performed according to custom or religious law.

SACRED Very holy.

SOLAR ECLIPSE The complete or partial hiding or darkening of the Sun by the Moon.

TERRACE A flat area created on the side of a hill typically used for growing crops.

THATCH Dried leaves or stems of plants used to make a roof or covering of a house.

WORLDVIEW The way someone thinks about the world.

Anderson, Michael, ed. *Early Civilizations of the Americas* (Ancient Civilizations). New York, NY: Britannica Educational Publishing and Rosen Educational Services, 2012.

Clint, Marc. *Aztec Warriors*. Minneapolis, MN: Bellwether Media, 2011.

Currie, Stephen. *Mayan Mythology* (Mythology and Culture Worldwide). Farmington Hills, MI: Lucent Books, 2012.

Dwyer, Helen, and Mary A. Stout. *Aztec History and Culture*. New York, NY: Gareth Stevens, 2013.

Laughton, Timothy. *Exploring the Life, Myth, and Art of the Maya* (Civilizations of the World). New York, NY: Rosen Publishing, 2012.

Macdonald, Fiona. *Hands-on History! Aztec & Maya*. Helotes, TX: Armadillo Children's Publishing, 2014.

Macdonald, Fiona. *You Wouldn't Want to Be an Aztec Sacrifice*. Rev ed. Danbury, CT: Franklin Watts, 2013.

Murphy, John. *Gods & Goddesses of the Inca, Maya, and Aztec Civilizations*. New York, NY: Britannica Educational Publishing and Rosen Educational Services, 2015.

Ollhoff, Jim. *Mayan and Aztec Mythology*. Minneapolis, MN: ABDO, 2011.

Pipe, Jim. *Mysteries of the Mayan Calendar*. New York, NY: Crabtree Publishing Company, 2012.

Raum, Elizabeth. *The Aztec Empire: An Interactive History Adventure*. North Mankato, MN: Capstone, 2012.

Schuman, Michael A. *Maya and Aztec Mythology Rocks!* Berkeley Heights, NJ: Enslow Publishers, 2011.

FOR MORE INFORMATION

Snedden, Robert. *Aztec, Inca, and Maya.* Mankato, MN:
The Creative Company, 2011.
Somervill, Barbara A. *Ancient Maya.* Danbury, CT:
Scholastic Library Publishing, 2012.

Websites

Because of the changing nature of Internet links, Rosen Publishing has developed an online list of websites related to the subject of this book. This site is updated regularly. Please use this link to access the list:

http://www.rosenlinks.com/ANCIV/Meso

A

agriculture, 9–10, 16–20,
  29, 38
arts, 35, 38–41, 42
astronomy, 35–36
Aztec, 15, 18, 19, 22, 24, 38
  population and cities, 15
  religion/gods, 14, 27, 28, 29,
    31, 34
  society/social classes,
    23–24

B

ball game, the, 24–25
bloodletting, 34
books, 38

C

calendars, 35, 36, 37
Chac, 29, 34, 41
Chac Mools, 40–41
Chichén Itzá, 14, 24, 32, 34
chinampas, 18, 20
Classic civilizations, 11–14
Cocijo, 29
colossal heads, 39–40
Cortés, Hernán, 15, 28

D

diet, 20–21

G

gods, 25, 26, 27, 29–31, 32,
  33–34, 40

H

Huitzilopochtli, 14, 29, 31
hunter-gatherers, 8

I

irrigation canals, 18, 20

K

Kukulcán, 31, 32

L

La Venta, 10–11

M

mathematics, 35, 36–37
Maya, 13, 24, 35, 36
  agriculture, 20
  art, 40
  astronomy, 36
  cities and population,
    13–14, 23
  mathematics, 37
  religion/gods, 29, 31,
    32, 34

11/16